Food Truck Business Handbook

A 21st Century Guide for Beginners to Plan and Run a Successful Mobile Food Business from Scratch

By

Forrest Rhodes

Copyright © 2021 – Forrest Rhodes

All rights reserved

No part of this publication may be reproduced, distributed, or transmitted in any form or by any means, including photocopying, recording, or other electronic or mechanical methods, without the prior written permission of the publisher, except in the case of brief quotations embodied in reviews and certain other non-commercial uses permitted by copyright law.

Disclaimer

This publication is designed to provide competent and reliable information regarding the subject matter covered. However, the views expressed in this publication are those of the author alone, and should not be taken as expert instruction or professional advice. The reader is responsible for his or her own actions.

The author hereby disclaims any responsibility or liability whatsoever that is incurred from the use or application of the contents of this publication by the purchaser or reader. The purchaser or reader is hereby responsible for his or her own actions.

Table of Contents

Introduction 9

Chapter 1 11

Food Trucking Basics 11

   History of The Food Truck Industry 11

   Pros and Cons of a Food Truck Business 15

   Daily Routine of a Food Truck Owner 21

Chapter 2 25

Initial Planning Considerations 25

   Naming Your Food Truck 25

   Food Truck Startup and Recurring Costs 30

      Estimated Startup Costs 31
      Estimated Recurring Costs 32
   Financing Your Food Truck Business 35

   Choosing Your Food Truck Location 40

   Finalizing Your Food Menu 43

      Choosing Your Food Menu 43

- Stocking Up On Ingredients 48
  - Tips on Proper Stocking of Ingredients 50
- Pricing Your Food Menu 52
  - Food Pricing Tips to Consider 52
  - Food Pricing Methods 54

Chapter 3 57

Develop Your Business Plan 57

- Executive Summary 58
- Company Description 59
- Market Analysis 60
- Organization and Management 61
- Service or Product Line 62
- Marketing and Sales 63
- Funding Request 65
- Financial Projections 65

Chapter 4 67

Follow The Rules and Regulations 67

- Setting Up Your Business Structure 67
- Hiring Employees 67

Get Your Permits and Licenses 68

    Food Service Business License 69
    Food Handler's Permit 70
    Hygiene and Safety Permit 70
    Gas and Electrical Safety Permit 71
    Commercial Vehicle License 71
    Driver's License 72
Getting Your Food Truck Insured 72

Zoning and Parking Restrictions 73

Chapter 5 75

Getting Your Food Truck 75

Food Truck Options 75

    Food Truck 75
    Food Trailer 75
    Food Cart 76
What To Consider Before Choosing a Truck 76

Chapter 6 81

Designing Your Food Truck 81

Choose The Right Vehicle 81

Operating Your Food Truck 83

Lay Out Your Food Truck 85

Mobility of Your Food Truck 89

Food Truck Branding.. 91

Bathrooms For Your Food Truck 93

Chapter 7 95

Checklist of Food Truck Equipment 95

Cooking Equipment... 95

Warming and Holding Equipment 97

Food Prep Equipment 98

Serving Equipment and Disposables 100

Refrigerating Equipment 102

Janitorial Equipment.. 104

Chapter 8 106

Food Safety and Food Poisoning Guidelines....................... 106

Chapter 9 113

Assemble and Manage Your Team 113

Determine The Number of Staff You Need...................... 115

List Their Job Description 115

Advertise Your Job Openings 116

Set Up Interviews 117

Begin Onboarding 118

Chapter 10 120

Marketing Your Food Truck Business 120

Branding 120

Website Development 121

Social Media Marketing 123

Food Presentation 128

Food Truck App 129

Location Strategy 131

Catering 132

Partnerships 133

Merchandising 134

Chapter 11 137

Common Food Truck Mistakes To Avoid 137

Conclusion 145

References 147

Introduction

The food industry is dynamic on its own; several modifications have been developed from the industry over the years. These modifications include the mobile food industry. This industry is more than a century old and has never stopped advancing through those long years. Food truck is becoming a really big deal in many areas.

However, as exciting as all of these can be, owning and managing a food truck business is no small task. It involves many tough labors you might not have thought of. To be successful as a food truck business owner, you need all the knowledge you can get on the business, its growth, and management. You need to be adapted to or be ready to adapt to hard work.

Sometimes, when the market starts to fluctuate, things could go really bad, and keeping your food truck business amidst the storm is not the easiest thing you would ever do. However, if you are keen on taking up a challenge and showing your culinary skill to the world, you can establish a successful food truck business.

In certain locations, this business is regulated by real tough laws and rules. You have to learn to keep to these rules or lose your business to the government. You also have to be really tough against the competition and stick your head through all of it. If you can do all of these things, you can grow this business into any size.

Without further ado, let's dive quickly into the ins and out of the food truck business.

Chapter 1

Food Trucking Basics

History of The Food Truck Industry

The food truck industry started in 1866 by a businessman named Charles Goodnight. He was involved in the ranching business, and by all records, he was the best of his kind in Texas and its environs. The young man was greatly admired by many for his great character. However, like every other person, he still had his habits. At 91 years old, he was addicted to smoking cigars. His addiction was so much that he smoked over 50 cigars in a day. Not long before his 92nd birthday, he married a nurse in her mid-twenties. You might be wondering how all these abstract details happen to be related to the subject at hand; food trucking.

Charles was a very determined man known for his diligence and hospitality. It was as though he had a strange charm. Before his death, Charles left a legacy, a legacy that has influenced the lives of many, a legacy that invented the concept we are considering in this book.

He invented the food truck business formerly regarded as the chuck wagon. The chuck wagon now food truck started as a mobile kitchen and culinary service. It was the first of its kind. It is no small wonder how this invention that came about several years ago has remained relevant even to this day.

This idea first came to Charles in 1869 while he embarked on a long journey. The common means of transportation at that point, especially when it had to do with long trips, was rail. Fortunately, or unfortunately, when Charles was traveling, he couldn't access the rail for some reason. Hence, he had to devise another means. As an innovative person he had always been, he found an old wagon once possessed by the army to sustain surplus resources. After modifying it to suit his comfort and make his journey smooth, he equipped the wagon with everything he could think of, ranging from shelves to kitchen utensils, barrels for water, firewood, and every other thing to ensure his comfort. He also took along preserved food items like dried meat and fish, rice, corn meal, beans, etc., while resorting to gathering fresh stuff along the way.

The revolution that birthed food trucks came about in 1872. After Charles returned from his journey, the food truck idea was sold out and it became a thing. People could travel miles with their own culinary equipment and food stuffs to prepare their own meal throughout their journey. Not long after, people began traveling with food in their trucks to another location to distribute or sell to the people there. However, food stand was still a foreign idea until a certain businessman wore curiosity like a cloak. He made a makeshift of a food stand by building with a covered wagon. He drove the wagon to a local newspaper office and modified it to suit his ideal model of food stand. The only menu he had at the time was pie and coffee, which happened to be the most conventional meal and the commonest meal ever purchased.

In 1894, other business-minded individuals started the sale of sausage in universities. The first university to establish the sale of sausage in food stands was the Ivy League university. More snack vendors came up as time went by. They were mostly located at construction sites and army bases, basically anywhere a large number of men were gathered. By 1936, there were more food vendors than there have ever been. Oscar Mayer started out a mobile hot dog truck. The truck he used was the Weiner Mobile. It was one remarkable invention that changed the business of mobile food.

Around 1950, ice-cream trucks became a thing. Between 1960 – 1970, chip and taco trucks became common, especially around the Mexican environs. Back then, when food trucks were regarded as roach coaches, it was plainly basic and greasy. Today, it is amazing how much has changed and more menus have been made available on the food truck vendor.

The menu includes all manner of savory fast food and snacks. The food truck has grown from being a workman's best meal to a professional treat that is enticing to everyone irrespective of positions or qualifications.

How did it all get to this point, you might be wondering? The game-changer was in 2008 when a group of food industrialists started selling barbeques. They never had a stable location; they were known for always moving from location to location. The only means of ever getting to track them was through social media. They had the practice of announcing their future locations to interested persons. Surprisingly, they always met the crowd wherever they were selling that day. People were always on the lookout for their location announcement. They presented a savory offer and treat than every other food vendor in town. They introduced new delicious, tasty, quick lunch that was also amazingly affordable.

Food trucks grew widely with the invention of the smartphone. There were several innovations like the NYC food truck, the Toronto food trucks and many others. Blogs and festivals were initiated that kept people informed on the practice of food truck tracking. This allowed people to explore various food truck delicacies and available varieties. In no time, food truck technologies were invented to help people manage their businesses. This technology was adopted by food truck owners and consumers. In no time, people began to use online payment, tracker apps, and loyalty programs to grow the food truck business.

Indeed, the growth of the food truck business is attributable to the inclusion of technology. It has grown from just a truck business to a total revolution. This revolution has been well seated in the western culture for almost a century. There is no telling what the next revolution holds in the food truck business.

Pros and Cons of a Food Truck Business

International records have it that the food truck industry has grown massively in the past years. At present, the industry is worth over $1 billion! Who would believe that such a shady invention would hold this much relevance even in the present world. Asides from providing fast food, it has grown to the point of employing close to 15,000 people actively.

Well, just like every business has its strain and possible disadvantage that even the strongest business plan cannot crack, the food truck has its own challenges too. It takes more than a strong business strategy and fundamental understanding of the business world to make your business skyrocket and soar. Doing business is hard enough, talk more of a situation where you have to maintain success over time. Hence, before you start to consider establishing a particular business, you have to familiarize yourself with the pros and cons of the business, so that you know what to expect.

Pros

1. It allows for innovation:
   Food truck business allows you the privilege to modify your business to suit your innovations. Unlike western restaurants, which are mostly conventional and maintain established menus over time, as a food truck vendor, you can decide to switch your menu at any time and organize your menu to suit your plan. You can draw up

your own line of menu from a family recipe to the trending food creation on the web. The freedom to build up your own menu list is an advantage that cannot be overemphasized.

2. It allows for entrepreneurship:
   If you've ever had the desire to own your business or put in practice basic entrepreneurship skills, the food truck business is just the perfect option for you to try out. As a vendor, you don't need anyone to administrate and oversee your decisions. You call the shot and do it your own way, your own style, your own time. You are your own boss. Another savory thing about being a boss is that there is really no one committed to sharing your earnings with you. Your earnings are your earnings alone. The motivation and drive come directly from the satisfaction you derive from the business, even if the bucks aren't coming in heavy.

3. There is less risk, unlike owing a conventional restaurant:
   It is also an opportunity for you to show off your cooking skills and make money without risking s much. Small businesses help to minimize risk.

This is a top advantage that is available to all startups. The lesser the capacity of the business, the less risk involved. If you're looking forward to being a restaurant owner, you'd have to graze the easy side and start as a food truck vendor. Success as a restaurant owner is dependent on the individual's ability to manage smaller risks the food truck business exposes them to. There is less startup cost demanded that a loss won't shut you off totally; you could always gather more capital and come back.

With consistency and the right amount of effort, you can watch your business grow from nothing to an empire.

4. It exposes you to boundless opportunities.

   The opportunities available in the food truck business are usually underestimated. With the internet, there are even much more opportunities you can take advantage of. Using the various available media, you can market your business easily. Also, you can move your business to different areas before deciding where to settle. This is the top benefit in managing a mobile business, and you can test many waters around until you find the water. You can experiment with festivals, outdoor event centers, or open fields; the alternatives are boundless. There is always a unique way to reach your target audience.

Cons

1. The workspace is small and limiting:
   This is one of the discouraging factors that prevent people from desiring to own a food truck in place of a restaurant. Culinary service can prove really stressful when the workspace is tight and small. It could be really limiting, except you discover what to do with the small space and utilize it maximally. With kitchen sets, pos system, and culinary tools in one place, there is little or no space to move about freely without clustering with something else. If you have a phobia for closed-up spaces, then a food truck business might not be the best bet for you.

2. Local zoning laws can be limiting:
   As a mobile business, you can be easily affected by zone restrictions. In certain places, you can't park your vehicle anywhere without getting yourself a fine. There are restrictions that could

limit you from harnessing certain opportunities. To avoid this limitation, you might have to schedule your locations in advance and send requests for a permit early. Some locations do not allow food trucks to use their parking lots more than once in a row. Also, food trucks would have to pay for space, just like cars. Hence, asides from scheduling and securing a spot in time, you also need to budget for parking space.

3. The need for constant repairs and maintenance: New trucks are extremely expensive, and it takes a lot of time for a low-income earner to make enough money to buy a new truck. Hence, most vendors go for second-hand or fairly used trucks and spend a little extra to remodel them into a solid good-looking food truck. Also, there are legal standards for constructing a fo/l.wqod truck in some developed places, so you have to find these out before purchasing or remodeling your truck.

After purchasing a truck, whether new or old, endeavor to save up a little money for repairs. You could act smarter and take your vehicle for period servicing to prevent the vehicle from breaking down, as repairs can be very costly.

4. Harsh competition:
The mobile food industry is now highly competitive than it was several years ago; with each passing time, the competition gets tougher. If you don't have a unique menu or a good customer relations attitude, you might have difficulty getting around. As much as it is a good thing that there is a high demand and value for food truckers worldwide, this could pose a huge challenge to the food truck owner.

Daily Routine of a Food Truck Owner

Running a food truck could be quite a task. It is not a job option for anyone who is uptight, neat freak, and lazy. Food trucking can be one hectic, difficult and dirty task. When your tire is flat, you have to take pride in repairing it or get someone to do so. It demands that you have to work for long hours, standing for most of the time. As a food truck vendor, you are not just a culinary expert; you are also expected to be a mechanic, accountant, and everything that has to do with owning your own business.

Everything spells hard work and more hard work. Even when you have staff working for you, you can't get out of the forefront; you still have the responsibility of setting the example for them and monitoring their work progress. In most cases, it is a long 9-5 job.

In developed countries, food truck owners have their schedule divided into 9:00-12:00pm, 12:00-12:30pm, 12:30-5:30pm, 5:30-6:00pm, and 6:00-2:30am. This doesn't represent the stereotype lifestyle of every truck owner, but on a scale of 1-10, every 9 truck owners have the same long schedule or similar.

9:00 am – 12:00 pm

Like every disciplined person, you rise out of bed at the sound of the alarm just before 9 am. Mind you; you have to be disciplined as a truck owner. This discipline doesn't just demand you to rise up early, you also have to be keen enough to go over your calendar and plan your day's activities, so you don't get caught up in a whole lot of unnecessary things. This should last for about two hours. Afterward, you should prep yourself and ensure your vehicle is in good shape before heading out to meet your teammates.

12:00 pm – 12: 30 pm

Within this time, you meet with your team members and go over the plan you must have drafted before setting out. Endeavor to pay attention to every detail and suggestion they have to share. You might get information from the news that you happened to miss at one point or the other, probably from the news, from customers, blogs, or competitors. This little activity helps everyone stay connected and abreast with their expectations and the task ahead.

12:30 pm – 5:30 pm

At this time, the team members head out to the market or bakery to purchase items for preparing the food on the menu. They do this with the list you must have given to them. Note that documentation is essential in food trucking to run an organized business. After getting each of these individual ingredients, they set to prep them. This involves slicing the vegetables, chopping the fruits, blending and grilling every necessary stuff. Other staff not involved in this activity is expected to get the truck ready and organized for business. Also, notifications should be dropped on all social media platforms to inform people of the chosen location for selling that evening. They should also carry out the necessary checking and correspondence while the food is being prepared.

5:30 pm – 6 am

It is time to unpark your truck and get out there from the kitchen to your first stop and other stops.

6:00 pm – 2:30 am

This is the trading window for all food truckers scattered around Europe. It is the time to show off your menu and wow the community with your unique dishes. You must have decided your destination before setting out. Ensure to drive carefully and gently not to spill off your food content. After arriving at your destination, remember the aim is to get the crowd of people, not just to make an impression. The larger the number of people, the higher the bucks. It could be overwhelming when you arrive at your destination to find a large number of people waiting for you at the destination before you arrive. You have to be well prepared for this moment; this is why you need to get everything prepared before setting out. The more relatable your services are the more people that are indited to patronize you.

Chapter 2

Initial Planning Considerations

Naming Your Food Truck

This is one of the most important things you must consider before setting out as a food truck business person. If you look back to your childhood or neighborhood, you would relate to certain names of vendors you can still remember even if you haven't seen them in a while. That's how powerful naming is. No matter how great your menu is, if you don't name your food truck correctly, you might be endangering and jeopardizing the future of your business. The success of your business is tied to the name of your business and the branding you give it. Your business branding generally includes the food menu, the required licensing and registration, and the business's name. Your name has to be a reflection of your business brand, and the name has to be remarkably linked to your food menu and the kind of business you intend to run.

Here are a few tips on how to name your food truck correctly;

- Pronounce the menu you intend to present:

Can someone relate to your business by just hearing the name of your business? People don't have the nerve to guess what your business is about as they come across it. Hence, you have to ensure that you add the name of your chosen food type in your business name. For instance, Enigmatic Gizzaria. People wouldn't have to think too deeply to realize that your business is centered on selling gizzards.

- Make it remarkable and brief:

This calls for a little creative twist. For people to remember your business name, it has to be outstanding and unforgettable. Something that would leave a long-lasting impression on your customers. Something people can easily identify and relate with even when they find it online or any random place.

- Ensure it is pronounceable:

After coining the name, is it something you can easily pronounce? I tell you, it can be quite frustrating after taking the time to coin a really creative name, and then you can't get people to pronounce it, well not like you can pronounce it yourself. The result of this is that you will have to keep reminding your consumers, suppliers, and colleagues of your business name. As much as you are trying to decide on a really creative name, ensure it is also pronounceable.

- Keep it short and captivating:

Names like Randy Raffle Royalty Sausage could be quite a mouthful for just a business name. Try to keep the name simple and, if possible catchy all the same. Long names are quite awkward and uncommonly irritating to people. Don't use more than three words in creating your business name.

- Avoid controversial business names:

There are certain names people find offensive. If you think deeply you will recall one or two offensive business names you have come across and how they put you off. You just have to avoid these names at all costs. Names that seem racial or discriminatory like Negro's asscream or something like that.

- Ensure the name has not been registered or submitted for registration:

You can get penalized by the law in some locations if you go ahead to register your business with an already registered name. Locally, people could also get vexed with you and start to attack your business if you fail to graze this path carefully. No matter how much you love a name you have coined, once you realize that someone has it already, whether the person is in the food business or not, you should avoid it as you could be endangering your business name, assets and customer bank if you chose to go ahead on it.

- You could make it a family name:

You can modify your brand name and add the names of your family to make it a household name. Adding + Co makes your brand look unusually professional. You can use + co to add location or family members.

- Use very familiar terms that a person could easily relate to:

Ambiguous words could pose a big problem to your business and can be quite challenging for your consumers to adapt to. Don't try to smash two big words together. Ensure to use simple words that people could easily relate to.

- Make a long list of the names you are considering:

You can make this list through any search engine and make sure to gather close to 100 names so that you have a large variety of options to choose from eventually. No matter how unlikely they might seem, note all of them and carefully select through them until you select at least 10 names.

- Conduct a survey:

You also need to conduct a name survey. After you have gotten the list of the names you are considering, create a mini-survey to let people select the name they feel is best. You can ask them to rate on a scale of 1-10. You can involve your family in the survey; just get them to pick the most unique names of all.

- Avoid using geographical names:

This could limit you from expanding your business as you might want to. When you are building an online presence, it is also important that you make the name location-neutral so that people won't associate you with a particular area.

- Select a peculiar business name:

In the former chapter, we have already established that competition is an unavoidable occurrence, especially in food festivals and roadside markets. This is a strong reason why you should get a name that stands you out from the public and makes you appear considerable to your customers.

- Think it through thoroughly:

Even after considering all the above-listed factors, ensure to think it through. You can't name your business twice; you have to select a name you are sure you would be sticking with through the years. You would be making expenses on branding t-shirt, logos, and food packaging. It would make no sense to change your business name after setting up your brand.

Food Truck Startup and Recurring Costs

When it comes to starting a food truck business, you have to be financially conscious. Some persons make the mistake of making ambiguous assumptions about the expected budget and estimated cost they are to incur in establishing their business. From any location you choose, you would spend nothing less than $40,000 in securing equipment and business assets. Depending on your location or business model, your capital might hit around $200,000. Some of the basic equipment you would need to acquire asides from the truck is your cooking appliances.

Before you purchase your truck, you have to decide the model of the truck you need; new or fairly used. Note that new trucks cost far more than fairly used trucks. Mobile Cuisine presented a table where they listed all the things you need to acquire before starting up your food truck business and a rough analysis of the cost.

Estimated Startup Costs

Food Truck Items	Estimated Cost ($)
Food truck	5,000 – 125,000
Vehicle inspection	100-500
Retrofitting	25,000-50,000
Generator	1,500-10,000
POS software	500-1,500
Paint	1,000-3,000
Truck wrap	2,500-5,000
Initial food supply	500-2000
Utensils and packaging	500-2,000
Website design	500-3,500
Office equipment	200-1,000
Advertising & public relations	500-2,000
Legal fees	500-2,000

Estimated Recurring Costs

Food Truck Items	Estimated Cost ($)
Payroll (4 staffs)	1,500-3,500
Commercial Kitchen & Commissary	500-3,000
Monthly Credit Card Processing Fees	Around 3% of sales
Fuel	250-400
Insurance	5000
Permits & Licensing	50-10,000 based on the location
Total Estimated Costs	**$40,000-200,000**

It could be difficult to raise capital for starting a food truck. This is why there are different price ranges available to you as a business person; you have to select the most favorable and affordable one before settling. However, you have to set up your business plan so you can start to hit your goal. Some financial agencies might request your business plan before they issue you a loan. Hence, you have to have your plan well mapped out with the amount you can afford. Some available options are;

- Equipment loan: if you have a good record of honesty and integrity, truck sellers could provide you with a loan to buy the truck.

- Rollover for business startups: as a retiree with more than $50,000 in your account, you can roll over the money in your account into your business as capital instead of going out to borrow. It is just like borrowing from yourself.

- Leasing: if you are low on funds, you can consider leasing a fairly used truck to startup your food truck business. There are different packages of leases; you just go through the itinerary and choose the one that works best for you. Some leases allow you to pay at the end of the week, month, or quarter. In contrast, some leases would allow you to use it for a long time until you can afford to buy it.

- Microloan: microloan are loans that are lesser and smaller in size than normal business loans. However, they might be enough to cover all your expenses; you could use them to support the capital you have at hand.

- Crowdfunding: with the internet, crowdfunding is very much easier. You only have to be creative with your business ideas and present them in an appealing way that is enticing and encouraging to the public.
- Personal loan: you can secure loans on your account if you have up to $50,000
- Business credit cards: if you have a good debt-paying attitude, a business credit card can be a good option for you.

After gathering funds for your business, you have to draft a well-detailed plan on how the money will be partitioned and distributed to meet your expenses. Make detailed financial projections before you start; it will help you to use your funds wisely.

One of the amazing solutions they came up with is food truck loans. These are loans specifically for food truck owners. They analyze your budget and give you money to acquire assets for your business, like a food truck and inventories. They also help you with finances for your marketing; you can say it is a wholesome loan.

Financing Your Food Truck Business

There are different options for financing your food truck

These options vary in terms of requirements, loanable amount, and the interest on the loan. Hence, you have the chance to compare between options to identify the one that works best for you. Some of these loans have been highlighted above; they will be discussed extensively below to help you make the best choices.

- Equipment financing:

This loan is open for individuals who want to start up a food truck business and buy equipment. The lender loans the individual a stipulated amount of money to buy equipment like an oven, food truck, deep fryer, and other major equipment. The borrower is charged very low-interest rates and repay the loan in due time. Failure to repay the loan early will cause the lender to sell the equipment to regain his money. Hence, the equipment financing can be said to be unique because the equipment is the collateral and the interest rates are fairly low.

- SBA microloans:

Small Business Associations Microloan is a lending program that allows borrowers a total sum of about $50,000 to purchase assets and employ as working capital. Interested persons would have to apply through an agent referred to as the microloan intermediary and prepare a collateral, alongside a personal guarantor. On rare occasions, they give out small loans like $13,000. This is a good option if you don't need a huge loan.

- Business lines of credit:

This is a different type of food truck funding as it doesn't give loans in a lump sum like other options. It is a loan-as-you-go option; you can make requests for money whenever you need to pump your working capital. You are given a duration to pay it back. In total, you are eligible to only a $100, 000 loan, also called line of credit. However, this amount varies in various districts. You can get within $10,000 to $1million anywhere. How this loan type works is this; you can take a loan of $5,000 out of the $10,000 you are eligible for and take another $3,000 when you need it. No matter the time difference between when you took the different loans, the loan is added together at the end of the day, and you are charged interest based on the timeframe to repay the loan.

- Business credit cards:

This is the best alternative for small expenses that you can easily pay off. However, it is the most expensive of the loan types, and it fits well for last-minute emergencies. For instance, you need to get new inventory to make a delivery; a business credit card could help you solve the issue on a clean slate. If you are very responsible with your finances and tend to return funds as at when due, it could earn you some points which you can convert to access reward programs.

- Crowdfunding campaigns:

This is a double benefit option. Using a crowdfunding campaign will enable you to make enough buzz about your brand on the internet and get people to come patronize you. Also, it helps you secure loans from kind-hearted, financially stable industries or individuals. There are established sites that allow you to raise money from professional investors who are in the business of funding startups. There are different types of crowdfunding; they come with different conditions. Some require that you pay back the money at a stipulated time. A few will only require that you give a sumptuous reward or pay in kind.

How to qualify for food truck financing

Every lending option has its own considerations for qualifying a borrower. Basically, to qualify for any loan, you have to be at least 6 months old in business and have a monthly revenue of $10,000. Also, in all cases except with equipment financing, you will be required to sign off a collateral. A good consigner would do you lots of favors.

For a food truck equipment loan, you might need to drop a deposit of about 5-20% if you are credit-worthy. In a more serious case, the lenders might require a UCC filing.

What credit score do you need to buy a food truck

Being credit worthy is a big plus to helping you secure a loan. However, every lender has their measurement of credit worthiness. Nonetheless, a credit score of 550 and 640 is the minimum credit score you should have as an intending borrower: the higher your credit score, the lesser your interest rate. Also, the lower collateral or deposit you'll have to make.

Will bad credit prevent me from getting food truck financing?

Having a bad credit doesn't sign you off totally from benefiting from a food truck loan. Different credit scores are entitled to different types or levels of funding. This is why you have to take your time to search online or locally for the options available to you; you will be surprised to find a food truck financing option available to your credit score bracket at a very fair rate. Loans like equipment loans are most favorable to low credit owners as it doesn't require collateral or deposits.

However, if you can take out time to build your credit, it will do you lots of good before going for a loan and help you save money in the long run.

Food truck financing rates and terms

As mentioned a couple of times in this chapter, loan rates depend on your credit worthiness and your loan option.

Every loan has different rates for different credit scores. With a very good credit score, you can get an equipment loan of several million dollars with a repayment period of 1-6 years. Annual interest could be around 3%.

For crowdfunding, there is no limit to the funds available to you; however, you will have to pay the platform you are crowd funding with. Also, there would require you to raise a particular amount in a certain duration; if you fail to accomplish that, you might not get access to a good loan.

In business lines of credit, the requirements are not so much. You should be eligible for a $250,000 loan with a 5% interest rate with a good credit score.

We've already discussed the terms surrounding credit cards explicitly. With an APR of more than 0%, your loan rates would be 13-20%. You would be expected to make an estimated minimum financial deposit of payments every month; if you limit yourself to these payments, your rates would definitely be higher.

Choosing Your Food Truck Location

Your food truck location is highly imperative to the success of your business. It determines to a very large extent, the level of turnovers that you would have in a particular period of time. In almost every street in the United States, there are crowds of food lovers that line up in the search for a unique and dynamic food menu. You have to be strategic in selecting your location so you can be positioned to find the right customers. Here are a few food truck location options;

Street parking: with street parking, you have to decide on your audience before you start scouting for spots. Are you on the lookout for mom, school students, or college staff? After deciding on your audience, it will be easier for you to choose a spot; the college parking lot, hospital, malls, construction sites, or offices. However, a major challenge will be getting a parking permit if you are in a very busy location.

Food truck parks: many food truckers run away from food truck parks because of the competition, unknown to them that they are running away from serious gold. Since the food industry evolved and expanded, many food truck owners have come to realize that working in collaboration is best for every one of them. This is because when multiple food trucks are lined up together, it attracts more attention and brings more customers. To get a spot here, you have to have a good professional relationship with well-to-do competitors. However, it is wise you look out for competitors with a non-competing menu. Their menu must complement your menu. If you sell ice cream, you should relate with a food trucker that sells doughnuts or sausage.

College campuses: this is one of the most convertible locations. School and college students love to be adventurous with food, so they will most definitely appreciate a food truck with a unique and superb food menu on their campuses. These campuses also tend to have events and activities like lunch and dinner hours to make huge sales. This is a super catch.

Business districts: if permitted, you can site your truck in front of major offices, especially during their lunch/break time. After getting a permit, you can give them an official notice of the time you'll be coming and what you'll be serving on certain days. This is a win-win situation for the business owner, the employees, and yourself. The business gets to satisfy its staff with this exciting food offer, and you get your bucks.

Farmer markets: this location is known to offer a good amount of food traffic. However, it is most effective for food prepared with locally grown resources and fresh produces. A menu that includes a fruit drink like smoothie will be a welcome idea.

Gas stations: in most parts of the states, gas stations are always busy, day and night. This is a very good traffic source that can boost your business. Although some gas stations do have a convenience store inside the management building, people would be glad if they are offered an alternative of buying from a close-by vendor.

You could also be of great service to travelers if your selected gas station is near a highway. Endeavor to get a permit before you park your vehicle.

Festivals and sports venues: festivals and events are very major highlights through which food truck vendors can make a lot of money. It is also an opportunity for you to introduce your business and wow your audience with an amazing mouthwatering menu that will make them search for you afterward. Renting a space at an event could be expensive, but you could still stand a chance if you park close to the venue.

Bars and nightclubs: night sales are very much guaranteed at bars and nightclubs because people are certain to become hungry after a long party or night out; you'll be a well-appreciated solution if you could secure a spot in front of a bar. To secure a spot, you only need to be friendly with the owner of the establishment and sell your idea on a mutually beneficial note to him, and the deal is sealed.

Finalizing Your Food Menu

Choosing Your Food Menu
It takes creativity and a little savviness to create your own food menu. Your food menu goes a long way to

affecting or defining your business brand and business strategy.

The very first step to take here is to decide the type of food you want to dish. In making this decision, you have to be mindful of your strengths and weaknesses. Not like and dislikes. This will help you navigate through the murderous competition in the market. Dwelling on your strengths will help you function maximally and fill an impending gap in the market. You can bring uniqueness to the market to give people a different idea of food truck business.

Choose the variety of food options; remember to keep it brief and unique except you intend to get help. Your food options should be closely related. Make a signature style by choosing a particular type of meal and sticking with it. You can still decide to come up with something out of the usual, and you can tag it as a "Special" so that your consumers can get an out of the normal experience. Also, make sure the required ingredients are something that you can easily access and can give your meal a taste of you. Be mindful that it is not every type of meal you can prepare in a food truck; make sure your menu consists of something quick and easy.

Making seasonal specials is a strategy most restaurant owners use to add uniqueness and variety to their menus. However, you have to have a constant before your special can carry great appeal. For example, you can decide to change your menu in a new season or add a special to suit the season, just like a chilled dessert in summer.

If you don't want to go out of the way to get new ingredients, you could just improvise or modify your basics, maybe try cooking them in a different style or serving them in a whole new fashion. This is a customer retainment strategy. It will keep them coming and coming because, just as they say, variety is the spice of life.

You can invent names for your product; that is the items on your menu. Don't just use flat names like chips or fries; add a mood to it. You could also make use of photographs to attract your customers. Only make sure you are not making empty hypes. Deliver as promised.

Some food truck owners miss out totally on the drinks adventure. There is an endless list of what drinks you can serve; coffee, sodas, wine, and bottled water. Add this to your menu, and your customer will have one extra reason to stick with you.

Popular food truck concepts

As stated in the introduction, food truck has grown beyond hot dogs to something much more captivating and interesting. Who would imagine! Today, cuisines and soups are served on the food truck. You could virtually source for any meal in the mobile food industry, and you won't be disappointed. People are getting really creative with their food concept. You can build yours and be bold about it. This is what will make you stand out.

Standing out is not as difficult as it seems; it only requires enough courage and boldness to make it happen.

Here are a few food ideas you can try;

- Barbecue; this is a common food truck concept and a popularly sort after one. You can source for more affordable ingredients and garner unique flavors to give it a new taste altogether. You can build a menu that would be customer satisfactory and pound wise.

    Paninis: paninis is a food concept that allows you to satisfy peculiar customer cravings; you can make different flavors and build a menu that everyone would love. You can give customers the chance to make a customized order.

- Desserts: after the ice cream trucks, dessert trucks are also popular. This menu option can be made to contain unique sweet and rich flavored ingredients to maintain the sweet tooth.

There are a variety of common desserts; you can experiment with new ways to make them and use them as a strong selling point.

However, endeavor to do a thorough market research, especially in your geographical location on the menu most food truck owners are selling. You don't want to be a photocopy of anyone, no matter how good what they do is. If you find out that a particular type of food you want to serve is already populated in the market, you can try a different spice or flavor on your own to give it a new taste and concept—something like crunchy waffles. You would have people lining up to try out what you've got. Another alternative is to go to a less populated market location.

Stocking Up On Ingredients

As a chef, stocking up is one very big task. You need to determine the quantity and flavor of what you are buying and buy according to need or description.

Also, after having created your menu, you need to stick by it in making your meal and shopping for your ingredients. Your menu is the guide to preparing your shopping list. If you shop without your menu, you will be stocking up many things that you don't need and running out of things that you need. You have a series of options to consider when deciding your stocking source—ranging from the wholesalers to the retailers. For each of these categories, you require a list to guide your shopping choices.

Also, note that even in the craze to deliver consistently, there are certain food ingredients you shouldn't gather in large quantities because they don't have the quality of staying fresh for long. You need to determine the quantity of everything you'll be getting, don't go ahead to bulk everything, or you'll find yourself putting it all out in the waste eventually. Here are some sources you can consider stocking up from:

- Wholesale food distributors: there are many distributors around that finding one won't be hard on you. You can make orders on their websites online and get them to deliver them to your house. You can ask around for wholesalers in your district or look out for food yourself.

- Manufacturers: getting supplies from manufacturers could be much more affordable and healthier for you. If you have a manufacturer around your area, you could as well take advantage of patronizing them. Although some manufacturers don't sell on retail to anyone, you might have to buy in large bulk from them. Most small manufacturing companies will be willing to trade their products to you. You could also subscribe to farmers that can provide you with fresh supplies.

- Local suppliers: there are surely food suppliers in every location. You can do an online search to connect with them and make them your source.

- Farmers markets: this is one of the cheapest sources you can take advantage of. You can be on the lookout for green markets. This will attract health and veg-conscious crowds. For some locations where farming is not so popular, it could be difficult to access a farmer's market geographically. You can search online for a market closest to your location and make your orders or drive across and shop through yourself.

- Shopping clubs: there are different categories of clubs that are indited in buying bulk food of good quality. Most of these clubs purchase these supplies and sell them at an affordable rate to restaurant owners and food vendors. Club members are required to pay an annual fee to retain their membership.

- Food cooperative: this is an association of food vendors with mutual benefits of getting supplies for their business. Unlike some organizations that contain competitive entrepreneurs, food cooperatives are noncompetitive. If there is no cooperative around your area, you could share an interest form to entrepreneurs around your area to form one.

Tips on Proper Stocking of Ingredients

1. Prepare and organize a storage section:

It is imperative that you set up a storage layout before purchasing stock or risk running out of space after buying your supplies. The size of your storage section should limit the number of stocks you should gather. You can minimize the number of equipment or limit the size of the equipment you'll get to make out space for taking in new supplies.

2. Track inventory:

You could keep track of the number of ingredients you use to prepare your food menu to measure the quantity of supply you need for a certain period.

3. Selecting suppliers:

As listed below, you would realize that there are many options you have when it comes to selecting suppliers. Evaluate these options carefully, how much do they charge for the same quantity of supply, which option has the best quality? These are evaluations you need to make before selecting a supplier.

4. Prepare your order ahead of time:

After making out space in your storage section, endeavor to make your order and send it to your suppliers early so you could get supplies at a cheaper price or a better quality.

5. Do away with wastes:

Never trade quality for quantity. While considering quality, make sure to also consider convenience and options for delivery.

Pricing Your Food Menu

Food Pricing Tips to Consider
- Cost of Food: your food cost is made up of the cost of ingredients it required to make a meal. The cost of meals differs based on the varying cost of ingredients of the different meals. Buying organic, sustainable ingredients could increase the price of your food. You can determine the costs of the meal on your menu, breaking the costs of your ingredient that each menu would require. Also, you would need to estimate the cost of the difficulty of the meal you are making and the time it requires you to make the meal.
- Other costs: the other costs that you need to check are the cost of equipment, cost of recruitment,

rent, and supplies. You can place the price of your products based on the costs it involves.

- Market changes: the market is always fluctuating due to certain unforeseen circumstances. The price of vegetables changes with the season. Same with other products. Make sure to fix your price at a flexible point where unstable market changes cannot affect it.

- Customer base: you would want to build a consistent customer base. Keep your eyes on the quality of value your target customers will be expecting. Every well rational customer will request value for their little buck of money. Are you sure you are up to the task? Also, monitor your customers' reaction towards your product; it will give you a concrete idea of how well to draft your prices.

- Competition: the mobile food truck has attracted a lot of customers over the years. This has led to a form of tough competition that could be quite challenging to defeat. You could use this as an advantage to influence your price and upscale in the industry. Check out your competitors' prices in your area before fixing your price. If favorable, you can decide to reduce your price.

Food Pricing Methods
- The most common method used in calculating the pricing of food is the food cost percentage pricing method. To calculate the prices of products with this method, you need to have your actual food cost and the target food cost percentage.

You would have something like food cost ÷ target food cost percentage = food price.

Take, for example, you have a barbeque on your menu, and the cost of making it is $1.50. This means that the cost of the whole ingredient you use is $1.50, and your target food percentage is about 35%. To achieve the selling cost of this food, you have to do the equation below;

$1.50÷0.35=$4.30

Percentage	Food cost	Menu price
20	$1.50	$7.50
25	$1.50	$6.00
30	$1.50	$5.00
35	$1.50	$4.30
40	$1.50	$3.75

Food cost is a part of the equation here. However, this formula is incomprehensive as it doesn't consider operational costs. Note that the more expensive your food costs are, the less you'll gather.

Another alternative is to use factor pricing to calculate food prices.

This means that you have a factor price fixed already for your food. In this case, this cost is representing the food-cost percentage. To achieve the factor pricing of this method, you need to divide the cost of food by the food pricing. This is the formula you can use to calculate the pricing factor;

100 ÷ target food - cost percentage = pricing factor.

Afterward, you multiply it by the food cost. Here's what you'll have;

Food cost × pricing factor = menu price.

Let's take an instance with this example. Let us take, for instance, that your target food-cost percentage is around 30%. Divide the 30% by 100%; what you will get will be around 3.33. Let's estimate that the cost of food is $1.50; you can calculate your pricing by doing the calculation below;

$1.50 × 3.33= $5.00.

Note that this method is very limited because it fails to take higher consideration of costs than others. This method can hike the price of food items and reduce the price of low-cost items.

Chapter 3

Develop Your Business Plan

The first step to establishing your food truck business is preparing your business plan. A business is very important in starting your business because it helps you secure funding from your investors. Ensure to prepare a business plan before you even consider getting assets together like your food truck.

One of the first things that you should consider when preparing your business plan is your vision and goals, the kind of food you'll sell, your location, required equipment and means of raising capital.

Gathering all this information could be a little overwhelming. This is why an outline has been created for you to easily itemize every one of your plans constructively to make coherent meaning to anyone who picks them up. There are several types of outlines; however, a good outline should cover transactional, operational, and financial plans. These plans are divided into the following;

Executive Summary

The executive summary is just like your introduction page. Hence, it has to be really impressive and convincing at a brief arm's length. This is the chance for you to elaborately talk about your company, its objective, its exponential growth rate, and the strategies devised to achieve success and higher growth.

This is where you get to sell your company by highlighting the imperative importance of your company's services to society and the gap it fills in society.

In conclusion, your executive summary should highlight;

- Type of food you intend to offer
- Geographical area of business
- Need for this business type or estimated solution
- Projected working capital and estimated period profit
- Future goals and projections for the business

Company Description

This section allows you to give explicit details of what your company is about, the business idea, and how you intend to grow it. It exposes your motivational drive to start up the business and possible positioning in the market. Here is where you explain your brand and relevance in the market. Basically, this is like the extended part of the executive summary where you discuss all the highlighted points.

Here are a few things you can consider giving details on in your food description;

- What type of food truck would you be using? Model and design.
- Reason for deciding on the food truck business instead of other forms of kitchen?
- Where will the food be prepared, in the truck or in a kitchen?
- Competition strategy in chosen geographical location
- Chosen consumer niche
- Qualities that stand out as a competitive advantage.

Market Analysis

Like the section indicates, you run a little analysis on the market situation, summarizing it with the reason for you choosing the market and how you intend to fill in a patch in the market and make it wholesome or better or influence its growth. Hence you need to do quality research on your market and the industry at large to gather facts to back up your claims and research findings to suit your conclusion. You can create a solid market analysis using the following key information;

- Highlight the major trends in the industry, consumer choices, level of growth, producer, and consumer groups.
- Analyze consumer's and producers' demographic information, such as age group, sex, economic, and socio status.
- Potential challenges to the market and ways to handle them. Your target audience and their needs.
- Level of progressive market growth
- List and analyze your competitors and how your business idea proves as a tough contender against their strategies.

- List the limitations and analyze the strategies to deal with them.
- Government and organizational or industrialization codes of conduct and regulations.

Organization and Management

Organization is key in setting up a business and, more importantly, a business like this where you might require people to work with you in your management team. You have to create a plan to stay void of confusion and keep every hand on deck. A good management and organization plan will ensure effectiveness. This section is very essential, especially if you will be working with more than two people. You need to itemize the responsibilities of every staff and include the profile of the members of your management team in a well-detailed format. Also, you should state the benefits that come alongside those responsibilities. Creating a chart is the best way to keep in touch with the structure of your business. You have to ensure that the number of persons you have on deck is sufficient for the task you need them to handle for you. There should be an even distribution of responsibilities.

Here are a few things to include in the organization and management structure;

- Legal documents
- Owners and investors profile
- Type of ownership

Profiles of your team members;

- Full name
- Task/ responsibilities
- Employment history
- Salary
- Community involvement

Service or Product Line

This is the section where you detail your services and products. What kinds of ingredients do you intend to use in preparing your menu? How do you intend to expand the market? What are your wow strategy for your consumers and the general public? This is a full section for you to display your innovation and creativity by talking about the following;

- Type of dish to be expected
- Motivation and passion about this food.

- Your competitive advantage in the market\Organization of recipes
- Lifecycle of your product
- Brand new product into the market
- Do your target market know you
- Possible limitation in demand for your product

Intellectual property in regards to the product and service;

    A. Any secret recipes or trade secrets
    B. Any need for non-disclosure of facts to staffs

Consider the future

    A. Intension to change the menu
    B. Intension to develop new product
    C. Enlargement idea of owning more food trucks
    D. Means of expanding your reach.

Marketing and Sales

This is one of the most important sections of your business plan. You are not planning to cook everything for yourself. Hence, you need a well-articulated strategy on how to get your target customers to patronize you and keep patronizing. You need a strategy to convince people to try out your snacks to increase your company's turnover. There a thousand and one ways to do this. You just have to choose the option that is best for the market and best for you. So, in developing a marketing strategy, don't trade originality and unique selling point.

Key things to include in the marketing section.

    A. How do you intend to enter the market?
    B. Setting lower prices than competitors
    C. Offer a novel product

Growth strategy

- Hiring more workers
- Acquire and expand extra trading products
- Estimated number of working days in a year

Distribution strategy

- Sell straight from the truck
- Organize food truck fairs and community leaders

Advertising strategy

- Using mass media loyally
- Discounts and special offers or Free samples and Give-away

Funding Request

This can also be referred to as a letter for funds or a request for funds. After evaluating the type of equipment you need to start, you need to itemize all these estimates to arrive at a final decision on your funding source. Indicating or including this section points out the fact that you intend to request for funds. So here, you will indicate how much you need, when you need it, and your repayment strategy. There are so many options you can take advantage of. However, before selecting your funding source, conduct an intensive research to decide on the option that will work best for you. So here are a few things to talk about in this section:

A. Estimate of capital needed.
B. Means of imploring gathered capital
C. Means of repaying the loan
D. Potential benefits to investors
E. Importance or benefits of the funds to your business.

Financial Projections

Making projections from scratch can be almost impossible. You are still very fresh in the industry, and you might find it difficult to find your way around. This is the more reason you have to make projections. Your projections give you an idea of what to expect.

This will help you to set clear and concise financial goals as though you have gathered some years of experience; this is where you list your financial history. As a start-up, you can use your knowledge of the current market situation to estimate the profit your business is expected to make over a five-year period and how you will settle off your loans if you took loans. This projection should synchronize with the needed funds you stated in your letter for funds.

Chapter 4

Follow The Rules and Regulations

Setting Up Your Business Structure

Food truck business is just like any other business idea; hence you have to decide the structure you will be using. You the option of making it a sole proprietorship, partnership, or joint venture business. This structuring is termed incorporation, and it helps you to protect your personal resources from your business resources. It helps you to establish a clear margin on the resources and assets of the owner and the business.

However, incorporating a business can be a lot of stress; this is why individuals prefer to start up as a sole proprietor before becoming an incorporated firm. In most districts, registering as a sole proprietor requires just your business name and a small fee. It is usually a straightforward process you can complete on your own.

Hiring Employees

You might need to get an employee, except all you intend to do is a simple meal. You would need people to help you with the organization and customer care services of your business because truth be told, you can't function everywhere and do an excellent job all by yourself; you need someone at the forefront or behind the scenes.

Before you employ a person, you need to get an [Employer Identification Number (EIN)](#) and prepare the following documents; [Form 1-9](#) and [Form W-4](#). You also need to be confirmed as a law-abiding taxpayer. You will also be required to commit financially to worker's compensation and insurance.

Get Your Permits and Licenses

In developed societies, you'll need to get a permit before you can start operating as a vendor. This task is really dreadful because the requirements to secure a permit could be unending in many situations. Also, it differs in several locations. However, most of the general requirements include;

- Vendor license
- Vending unit permit
- Certificate of a sales tax authority
- Letter of recommendation or approval from food protection course exams for mobile food vendors

- Required food truck equipment

In most cases, you will likely have to renew this permit periodically. Whenever you are ready to make a renewal, your vehicle will be thoroughly inspected by the health department in your district. Do not forget that your vehicle will need to be registered with the vehicle inspection office. You need to get yourself a driving license if you would be driving yourself; if not, ensure your driver has a driving license. If your vehicle is huge, the driver might be required to get a commercial driver's license.

Now, let's take a deeper look at the different permits and licenses you will be needing

Food Service Business License

After deciding on the business type you'll be running, endeavor to register with the local district. After which, you'll need to get a business license that shows you are registered and licensed to run a food truck business in your chosen location. This is what gives you the right to go ahead and commence business operations in a certain environment.

When securing a license, indicate the type of business you are starting and your business's basic operations. If you are intending on circling about a niche, endeavor to indicate it in your registration document. Note that some districts might require that you renew your license every once in a while to keep it valid.

Food Handler's Permit

A food handler's permit is a document that allows you to launch your business as a verified food truck vendor. Your local district issues it, and upon passing the necessary examination. At the end of the examination, the vendor is given the permit to validate his food service to the community. Although the questions are basic, you can take trainings and courses to brush yourself up before taking the exam.

Hygiene and Safety Permit

After gathering all necessary permits and licenses, just before you set off, you need to get a hygiene permit to validate that your products are hygienic and safe for consumption. This permit will be renewed after periodic inspections. The inspectors are usually from the health department. Their sole task is to engage in rigorous analysis and search to ensure that the food truck maintains a standard level of hygiene, especially for food safety. This is one of the strictest permits to maintain even after acquiring it; your business could easily be shut down if the health officers discover any alarming or unhygienic practice in your business.

Here are a few checks they make;

- Manner of storage
- Staff are hand gloved
- Clean and neatly maintained cooking equipment
- Practices in accordance with safety and fire codes

Gas and Electrical Safety Permit

Most food truck vendors use gases and electricity in cooking. Hence, there is a need to secure a permit for security purposes. Before this permit is issued to you, a safety officer will help you validate your equipment to confirm if they are in tandem with the law. Also, they monitor your safety practices or hazard records annually. There are officers within your district that are in charge of making such assessments and issuing you a permit. Endeavor to comply with them and keep your electronics in accordance with the law.

Commercial Vehicle License

As I have already highlighted above, all public or commercial vehicles need to be licensed. Some states would go as far as requesting your driver's license before licensing your truck.

Driver's License

This is a requirement for every public vehicle because it is a compulsory requirement to commence food trucking in any district. It is not enough to have a license; ensure that it is valid and up to date.

Getting Your Food Truck Insured

As a rational business owner, it is wise that you get your business insured and compulsorily for you if you are a food truck owner. This is a necessity for a mobile business because the risks are highly consequential and limitless. As a food truck vendor, the insurance you are to take is divided into general liability insurance, commercial vehicle insurance, property insurance, general auto insurance, and workers insurance.

General liability insurance is necessary if you would be servicing large crowds in festivals or funfairs. Commercial vehicle insurance is the most compulsory and non-negotiable. Your business is exposed to many potential hazards like fire, accidents, and others; these hazards are covered by the vehicle insurance and property insurance covering your assets. Also, if you would hire the services of private individuals, the workers' insurance is a compulsory take. Finally, as a citizen, the insurance required by the states is termed general auto insurance. This insurance is estimated at around $2,400 every year. You can find out other required insurance options at the insurance office or on your state website.

However, insurance costs can be draining. If you might want to reduce the cost of insurance, here are a few factors that influence insurance cost; type of truck, district location, hours of operations, nature of business (seasonal or general), equipment types, and forms.

Zoning and Parking Restrictions

Zoning restrictions are everyday things in developed cities. These restrictions are sometimes segmented into commercial and noncommercial zones. They limit the mobile activity or presence in a particular environment. Most districts limit mobile businesses like a food truck to a mapped-out location which is not always favorable. In most places, you can find an online list of places that are open to parking and zoning and their requirements and places that are well restricted. You might be given a time duration to use a parking lot and required to pay an amount of money which is usually termed fair.

Before settling for a parking location, ensure to do thorough research about the available or negotiable space across your chose geographical location. You can visit your district vehicle office or a website. Some laws govern the situation of food truck businesses like every other business, for example, no food truck near the school area. Also, note that you are expected to park in such a way that your vehicle is totally out of the way, and you are not obstructing any vehicle from parking or moving out.

Chapter 5

Getting Your Food Truck

Food Truck Options

For anyone intending to start a food truck business, the available options span from trucks to trailers to carts. There are not so many options. However, for every option you select, you need to be well aware of what each of these options entails and what they allow you to accomplish.

Food Truck

This is the vehicle with the largest space option, and it is very flexible. If you want to build a creative magnifying kitchen empire, then you should consider using a truck. Its average length spans from 14 to 34 feet. This ample space allows you enough room to prepare your ingredients, make your meals, and even serve them.

Food Trailer

This vehicle functions like a food truck and a cart. It is similar to a truck because it allows you a good amount of space for cooking, serving and storage. Also, just like a cart, you would have to tow it to wherever you are headed. A food trailer is space and convenience functionary; it allows you to cook and serve a large crowd time after time.

Food Cart

A food cart is the most affordable option and easier to manage. It requires low maintenance and is very simple to move about. All it requires is for you to join it to your car or bus and tow it to your location. However, it allows very little space for working. It also limits the amount of food you can serve at a time in a day.

What To Consider Before Choosing a Truck

Before selecting any of these options, you need to decide on the following;

1. Your menu: your menu determines the processes you would have to prepare to engage in. prepare a list of the food ideas you are considering, make a list of the required tools and the processes involved. Also, decide on your storage options. Your menu should be deciding on the capacity you intend to start off your business. Do you intend to start small scale and increase your scale later? These are things to consider and use in structuring your menu.

2. Preparation location: there are two preparation options you have; on the truck and elsewhere. Elsewhere could be a commission or commercial kitchen. Preparing your food in a commercial kitchen is a lovely idea as it allows you enough space to do your work excellently and provide quick customer service. This is also supported by districts who disapprove of preparing meals on the truck for health reasons. Using a commercial kitchen would require a timely financial commitment and save you the stress of gathering equipment for your truck.

   Preparing your food at home is also a viable option. However, if you are considering any of these options, be certain that you'll need to garner strong storage appliances.

3. Truck cost: you have to be sure that the truck you are purchasing has a very good maintenance plan. Your vehicle has to be enticing and appealing to invite consumers. If your vehicle has a bad appearance, it might require that you paint it. Also, if your vehicle happens to have a maintenance issue, you will have a hard-long

work day fixing it. Hence, it would be best if you went for a brand-new truck that you can trust. If you don't have enough capital to see to that, you can consider equipment financing or applying for a lease.

4. Location of the business: it is no news that this is one of the most important things to consider before starting up a food truck business. However, you should also have in mind that your truck size could make your location unconducive. Some locations do not permit large trucks. Also, there are regulations for selling with trucks and carts in certain locations. Regulations for carts are stricter than trucks.

5. Number of employees: for a serious food truck business, you should be ready to hire at least three works to assist in the culinary and serving option. If you would have employees, you need a space that can comfortably accommodate every one of your workers.

The vehicle should give them enough space to move around and work effectively. Also, while commuting, you need to ensure that there are enough seatbelts for everyone.

6. Estimated number of customers: the number of customers you expect every day will help you select a solid storage space. You'd need to store up all your ingredients comfortably without stress and sufficient space to help you move your equipment. If you are estimating a large number of customers, you should not consider a cart.

7. Customer preferences: the business is aimed at satisfying a targeted group. You are to decide on this first of all. What caliber of customers do you think you are bound to have. What location are they sited? This will help you sharpen the texture of your business activities and your business branding

A Short message from the Author:

Hey, I hope you are enjoying the book? I would love to hear your thoughts!

Many readers do not know how hard reviews are to come by and how much they help an author.

I would be incredibly grateful if you could take just 60 seconds to write a short review on Amazon, even if it is a few sentences!

\>> Click here to leave a quick review

Thanks for the time taken to share your thoughts!

Chapter 6

Designing Your Food Truck

Choose The Right Vehicle

There are different steps people take to acquiring a food truck. You have the option of designing the interior of the truck on paper first and going ahead to get the truck before making a design. All of these options are correct in themselves. However, you need to decide on the layout before purchasing the truck. With the layout already available, you will be able to make a more wise and brilliant decision. Decisions on the type of truck that will allow for maximum space for your cooking and customer care activities and a truck that will allow you to layout your equipment in such a way as you intended.

This doesn't mean you would have to go all out looking for a food truck that presents your food truck in the model as you have drawn in your design. You might have to adjust your design after getting the truck in order to get everything in. Nonetheless, a structural guide will do no harm.

Unlike several years ago, when available food truck options were boring and dull, today, several food trucks options are open. It is not difficult to discover the food truck of your dreams. This is one of the biggest and consequential decisions you'll make in your journey of establishing a food truck business. Below is a short list of things to consider in selecting a good food truck;

1. The size: most persons go for bigger food trucks because it allows them to store enough equipment as they would and achieve sufficient space to function effectively.

2. Outlook: your food truck is the first signature of your brand; you have to ensure the exterior is clean and attractive.

3. New vehicle or fairly used: are you starting vintage in the next schedule.

4. Fuel: most vehicles use fuel in powering their activities. There are great options for vendors who would be covering rural areas like local fairs. However, electric cars are most cost-effective and much more sustainable, especially if you intend to cover long distances.

After deciding on the truck type you'll be getting, you can begin to make decorations and equipment selections to suit your truck. Note that your truck is the biggest asset you get to own as a food truck vendor; hence you have to be really careful when making a selection.

Operating Your Food Truck

Operating a food truck requires some form of expertise and equipment, some of which can be really expensive, but you need them, so there are no alternatives. This section will be addressing the powering options for your truck. Answer the following questions before choosing a powering option.

- What is the estimated voltage that your equipment will require?

- Are there power emissions regulations across your district? What are they?

- Does your insurance rate cover your source of power?

Generators: this is the most common power source in developing cities. There are different sizes and types of generators. Some consume more diesel than others.

Some are much heavier and tougher to manage. However, they are very solid and release a lot of power; you can carry equipment like freezers, fryers, and ovens at once. With a good generator, you won't have to worry about carrying all your electronic equipment and functioning maximally. You might have to worry about the carbon monoxide and heat your generator would be producing and how to diffuse it. One proven way to reduce the torture of these oxides is to ensure that you install your generator properly with a good ventilation allowance. You can use professional help and keep your generator away from flammables. Also, don't forget to save some money for fueling.

Solar panels: these are really good options if you intend to keep some bucks for savings. Solar panels can be really costly, but it is a sure investment to keep you from spending more money afterward except for maintenance. With good maintenance, you can use a solar panel for a very long time before it goes wane. The panels are pretty flat, and you can place them on the roof or on a good edge where they would receive a lot of sunlight. Deciding on the location to place your panel can be a really tough decision if you are mindful of your ventilation and truck aesthetics. With these panels fixed up, you don't have to worry about power except in winter.

Fuel-powered generators: this is an all-time power option you can trust in winter and summer. However, you would have to save money for consistent fueling after purchasing the generator. They release more emissions than the normal generator. However, you can save more money by going for a biodiesel generator; these generators can be powered with vegetable oil. That would save you a whole lot of money, especially in districts where fuel is expensive. Ensure to carry on with you extra cans of fuel or oil before embarking on a business trip.

Lay Out Your Food Truck

We have talked a little about layout when addressing the selection of truck type. Whether you choose to draw your layout before or after buying the truck, what is most important is that you have a layout. This is what guides you to making interior decorations and assembling your equipment. The organization and decoration of your truck will directly impact your business by affecting the comfort of your customers and staff. The major place in your food truck you should be very mindful about structuring is your kitchen; this is where you make the magic. So, you have to be really intentional about how you structure this place. A good kitchen layout could make your staff feel really good and professional as they work. A poor kitchen design would only dissipate all the passion and add up pressure to your work.

Your menu helps you in deciding on how to structure your kitchen. Also, your kitchen layout should be motivated by comfort, safety, and efficiency. Here are few checks to make;

- Strong, durable floors.
- Sufficient ventilation
- Adequate space for movement

- Emergency gateways
- Ease of storage

Your kitchen makes your workflow easy; design your kitchen with that in mind. Also, don't try to make your truck like someone else; always be keen on uniqueness. Here are a few things to make space for in your kitchen;

- Serving spot
- Clean up corner
- Handwasher
- Cooking area
- Fryers, grills, and stove
- Storage equipment like a refrigerator.

There is a lot to note when designing your food truck; this can be stressful if you are not a good multitasker or keen on details. You can lay this off your shoulder by outsourcing a food truck designer. Three are so many of them. Although outsourcing could cost you some extra bucks, it saves you stress and time. Now you have just enough time to fix up every other detail.

Service spot:

Most trucks make use of a service window. The size of this window is way dependent on the type of food you serve. You can also make good enough space for your POS system and every other thing you will need in serving. Your service point is an opportunity or an opening to make an impression on your customers. Take advantage of it and ensure your service point is always organized.

Ambiance: it is highly impressive to put a shed over your service point. It makes your customers feel relaxed and welcomed. This could really be a good turner in the summer period. Also, you can use different types of lighting to make decorations in your truck. Bright, colorful lighting could make your truck look inviting and irresistible to slurp by.

Mobility of Your Food Truck

Although food trucks are in the mobile food industry, some food truck vendors unindustrialized their business by choosing to stay put year after year. This option is open to anyone interested in the food truck business. You can stay in one location throughout the year if you wish; there is no penalty for doing that. It has its own advantage you might enjoy exploring. However, making such a decision would have a direct impact on your design.

When you choose to stay put, you pay for a spot as rent and positioning your truck in the space. However, that is not the only expense you will be making; you would have to provide a seating space with chairs and all, you would have to provide outdoor restrooms and make use of reusable cutlery. All these screams money! It is just like establishing a normal restaurant. The only difference is that you are selling from a truck. Here are modifications you would have to make in designing your truck;

- Small service window: you don't need a large serving spot anymore because people could sit to wait for their order while you bring it to them, or they sit waiting to pick it up. You can take up that extra space for your cooking activities.

- More sophisticated exterior decoration. Since you would be in that spot for a long time, you can spare the interior décor and do a very inviting exterior décor.

- Extra required storage space for cutleries; reusable cutleries could take a lot of space and also demand that you hire an employee to take care of them.

If you would be staying mobile, then you need to note the following;

- You need to have a well-organized storage space, so you can pack everything up as you move about.

- You also have to be mindful of the weight of your equipment and the number of staff you are moving with. More weight implies more fuel and wears of your truck. Consider moving with lightweight equipment and fewer staff if you will be going a good distance.

- Some vendors set up equipment when they finally find a crowd and a parking spot. Equipment like a garbage can and sandwich board. Any other thing that will be set up needs to be pretty simple to tear down. Don't carry about complex equipment for ambiance or décor; you could have a problem tearing it down after setting it up.

- You will need to carry on an extra of every necessary equipment to avoid being stranded. Take along with you a basic toolkit you can move about with.

Food Truck Branding

This branding section is to help you secure a place in the market with your own fair share of customers. Branding is also necessary for upscaling in the market. This is a peculiar situation because you are trying to attract customers. Hence, your branding needs to be top-notch for them to find you convincing and want to patronize you in place of a nice brick-and-mortar restaurant. Your truck exterior is also a strategy in getting people to want to buy from you. Here are few tips to making your exterior work like magic;

- Vinyl wraps

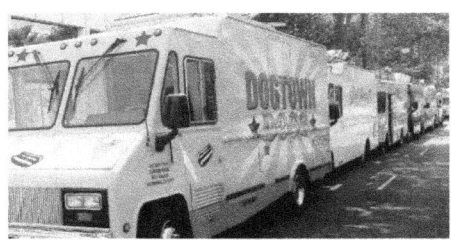

These are quite expensive designs that allow you to print any form of design on your vehicle; you can print on your logo or the image of the food you'd be selling. Endeavor to use a very bright and attractive color. This is the sure way to establish your brand identity and get people to know you. Although this is the most used exterior design option, it could really be expensive and difficult to install.

- Hand painting

A worthy alternative is painting your vehicle. This is a much simpler and cheaper option. With a good knowledge of painting or a good tutorial, you can paint your vehicle yourself. However, it could be difficult painting your logo or objects on the vehicle; a local artist could save you the trouble and make it look like it. Hiring an artist is a good way to spread the word about your business and make your truck stand out.

- A mixture of each

If you want your logo to be printed on your vehicle, you could use vinyl wrap to print out your logo and hand paint other parts of the vehicle.

Bathrooms For Your Food Truck

Depending on the district where your business is operating, there are a couple of regulations and modalities you'll need to consider when setting up your food truck bathroom. Besides this, you also need to consider your truck size, the location you are selling at, and what works for you.

In most cases, the only permitted bathroom function for a food truck is a washroom. However, if you are allowed to have a toilet in your truck, and you have the required space, it could go a long way to increasing your staff's comfortability and productivity.

Nonetheless, you would have to be well prepared to deal with issues like a grey water tank. Also, you've just added another cleaning shore.

Chapter 7

Checklist of Food Truck Equipment

In this section, we'll be looking at the different categories of equipment that you will need to run your food truck business

Cooking Equipment

Firstly, I need to establish that all of this equipment is important and useful in itself. You only need to decide on the different types of equipment under each category that you will be getting. To maximize the space in your truck, you need to get cooking equipment that has counters and shelves. Give enough space to the frequently used equipment and ensure to use of countertop appliances. Below is an intelligent list of the vital cooking equipment you'll need for your food truck.

- Grill: these are the most useful if you will be making items like pancakes, eggs, and burgers.

- Range: this equipment allows you to cook your sauce or proteins in any form you wish; frying, boiling and simmering.

- Microwave: an all-time saver and stress reliever to heat up food or steam vegetables.

- Toaster: you can use the toaster to give your bread or sandwich a thicker texture.

- Cheese Melter: in some places, this equipment is also referred to as salamander. You can use it to melt cheese; it also browns the top of foods.

- Fryer: an indispensable kitchen companion you can use in making all types of fries.

- Charbroiler: this works like a griller. However, it is basically to design your food by giving it grill marks on the surface.

Warming and Holding Equipment

This equipment is essential if you are looking to make your food truck a fast food stop point. They help you to store your food at a safe temperature. Safe here implies keeping it from foodborne illnesses and health violations. They hold this temperature for a very long time. Here are a few warmers you can consider;

- Countertop food warmer: this is a versatile warmer that helps keep real food like casseroles and pasta under good temperature.

- Fry dump station: this warmer is used to keep fries warm once they are straight out of the fry.

- Soup warmer: you can use this is keeping liquid food like soup warm until it is served.

Food Prep Equipment

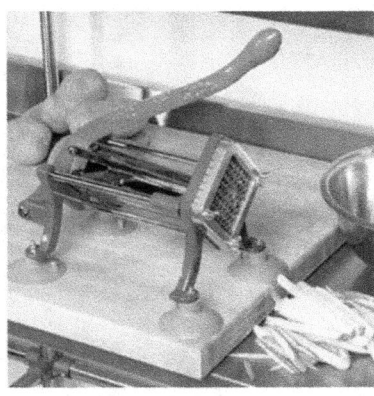

Here is another commonly used piece of equipment. There are so many of them. This equipment covers every piece of equipment and tool you use to prepare your food. They vary depending on your menu. Here are a few popular ones:

Stainless steel work table: if your truck size permits, you can consider getting a stainless-steel surface for additional workspace.

Cutting boards: also called chopping boards. This is one piece of equipment you can't go a day without. It is very helpful in cutting, chopping, and slicing.

Knives/ knives rack: a good knife will save you from keeping your knives carelessly. A good knife also preserves your efforts and energy. It allows you to make smooth cuts easily.

Skillet: these are very important tools for steaming and pan-frying.

French fry cutter: you can use this to cut your plantain or potato really fast without exerting energy.

Blender: also referred to as a food processor, it can be used in grating or liquefying vegetables or tomatoes. In most cases, it is used in making smoothies.

Thermometers: you can use this to measure and ensure that all your food is cooked at the right temperature.

Turners: these are versatile equipment used in making burgers and vegs.

Saucepans: just as the name depicts, it is very useful in making sauce. That is through all the processes involved; boiling and simmering.

Serving Equipment and Disposables

As a mobile vendor, it only makes sense that you use disposable serving equipment. Only make enough space for them in the truck storage unit. Also, ensure to carry enough supplies every day you set out because your business is automatically closed down for that day if you happen to run out of them. Here are lists of collections you need in your supply unit;

- Serving utensils: you need something to serve with. Ensure you always have a good and clean serving spoon.

- Condiment dispenser: you can position this close to your truck once you find a parking spot so people can help themselves with it. However, keeping it inside will help you monitor its usage.

- Squeeze bottles: you can put this on your service table for customers to put the condiments with their hands.

- Cheese shakers; this award-winning shaker is also used in shaking sugar and spice.

- Paper food trays: this is commonly used by fast-food truck owners. You can use it to serve dishes like snacks or quick food.

- Plastic dinnerware: this is a synchronizing option for large dishes.

- Plastic cups: plastic or paper cups are alternatives to serving beverages in bottles.

- Portion cups: you can package the condiments in portion cups, so customers get only the right amount for them.

- Paper napkins: this can be adopted on the service table, so people get to help themselves.

- Disposable gloves: this is a health-required tool for handling food.

- Aluminon food wrap: you can use this to wrap up ingredients you intend to use at a later time and keep it in the fridge or storage space.

- Guest checks: you can receive your customer's order on a form called guest checks. So you serve in an organized manner.

- Take out container: you can provide this for customers who intend to carry their food to a different location.

Refrigerating Equipment

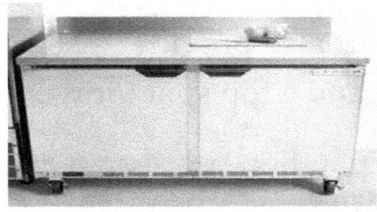

Having a refrigerator is really necessary if you would be preparing the food in your truck. This will help you store up ingredients in a fresh state. In most cases, vendors get a refrigerator for every section of an item they will be preparing. They could single out a refrigerator for basic ingredients, another to store in soda or beverages, and a small refrigerator for items like sauce. However, it is also possible to get a refrigerator that can allow you to store up all of these things at a go and save money plus space. You don't want your truck jammed up with refrigerators when you can have an all-service refrigerator. Here is a brief list you can choose from when regarding refrigerator;

- Worktop refrigerator: this is a type of refrigerator that comes with a sleek, smooth surface for working.

- Sandwich refrigerator: this refrigerator is mainly used in storing salad or sandwiches. It has a cabinet at the bottom where you can store the sandwich. It also provides a space for assembling your food and a top spot for working.

- Pizza preparation refrigerator: it could take a really long time to prepare the ingredients for pizza, and you could also lose the freshness of the ingredient if you prepare it long before you are ready to make it. A pizza preparation refrigerator helps to solve this problem. It allows you to store up your pizza ingredients and also provides a topping for you to work on.

- Glass door refrigerator: this is an excellent option for storing up canned drinks and beverages.

Janitorial Equipment

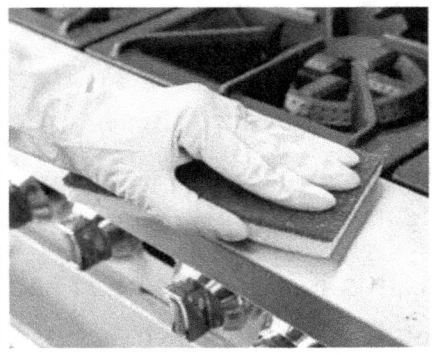

Food serving is a touché business; hence you have to be clean conscious and health effective to ensure your surroundings within the cooking and serving area are clean. You can't be given a permit to function as a food truck vendor without having a good janitor. Below is a list of janitorial supplies you need to store up;

- Three compartment sinks: you would need enough room to set this up. However, it is very functional and helpful for rinsing supply tools and dishes.

- Hand sink: the presence of a hand sink encourages hygiene amongst your staff.

- Anti-fatigue mats: these mats are also referred to as anti-slip floors; if you position them under your leg, they can help you hold a firm stand and avoid slipping while working.

- Sanitizing chemicals: these are detergents or chemicals that are used in cleaning. Hand sanitizers are a good example.

- Sponges: this is a tool used in scrubbing dirt off supply equipment or a work surface. It is mainly used when washing.

- Trash can: this is an indispensable need in your truck. It helps you to dispose of your dirt and trash easily. Every food truck is expected to have a waste disposal area; in that spot, you can fix in a trash can or bag of any model.

- Broom and dustpan: after cooking or serving, it is good hygiene to sweep the dirt with a broom and packing them to dispose of with a dustpan.

Chapter 8

Food Safety and Food Poisoning Guidelines

The presence of the food truck business has reduced the barrier to entering the food industry. Now, everyone who thinks they stand a chance in the kitchen can actually try their hands out with less cost, less stress, and proper training. The organizational structure is unique and makes them a sort after option for food service.

However, there are still limitations quite peculiar to the food truck business due to its small nature and mobility structure. Space could really be an issue in the culinary world, and in as much as you might be creative enough to handle the space, there are some unavoidable repercussions that you might have to deal with. First off, making a quality meal in such a situation could be quite challenging.

Also, the decreased space affects the quality and extent of sanitation. Unlike it is expected that the cleaning should be a lot easier because the space is small, the cleaning becomes tougher because you are cranking up several things in the same space.

This poor sanitation could lead to food poisoning if not well managed. Food contamination and poisoning could also be a result of human carelessness and negligence of safety practices.

Improper food truck management and safety

Although it is usually believed that the food truck business is the easiest form of culinary business, as much as this is true, there has also been a high level of failure with an estimate of over 60%closed down food truck businesses in their first year of operation.

Research conducted revealed that 27% of truck owners in Los Angeles were graded poorly by the health officers on food truck inspection. This goes a long way to point out that maintaining a healthy food standard can be a challenge for food truck vendors.

You might be wondering about the relationship between health reports and business progress. Here it is;

In some districts, vendors are expected to post their last inspection report on their windows. This is to guide consumer choice and protect them from consuming harmful or unsafe foods in the bid to satisfy their hunger.

Asides from the report presented, which indicates food truck hygiene problems could be really gross, and if not handled well, it could get dangerous. In most trucks, things like rodents' infestations and fesses were found. So far, this is the most disturbing unhygienic item discovered, and it is actually very common. Most truck owners are unaware of this and keep their spaces cranked up together without enough space for them to breathe. Another sad side to the story is that mobile food inspectors are very scarce, leading to only a few trucks being inspected.

Harsh reality of food truck maintenance

By now, you must have realized that the most challenging issue in managing a food truck is the size. That small size is the cause of several undoing. The business owners only have a contributory effect on the success of the mobile business.

It is not enough to gather all the required equipment in managing a food truck, you also need to be well skilled in making the best use of the limited space or risk getting yourself frustrated. The chef has little working space than a small personal kitchen. Hence, the janitorial management issue. Trucks that store their ingredients on a shelf or produce aboard could be exposed to rodent's attacks or infiltrations. This is because small cranked-up spaces give room for pests to breed and multiply. The consequence is that the food gets contaminated terribly.

Pest invasion is one of the most common sources of contamination. These contaminations, if not well managed, can lead to terrible illnesses. Below is listed other form of contamination and exposed risks;

- Poorly sanitized work surface.
- Unhygienic handling of food during preparations
- Improper refrigeration

These are really threatening risks that could pose serious health risks. It could be a whole lot of stress for the truck manager to decide on the safety of his products, except he is certain they are operating in line with the standard operating procedure.

Standard operating procedures

This includes a list of steps alongside the required functional tool in making food truck hygiene management easy. These steps are quite easy to follow, and they have been proven to be solutions to the hygiene problems of a food truck.

- Constantly wash your hands and dispose of your used hand gloves frequently: dirty hands are a very quick way to spread contaminations and cause illnesses. You must wash your hands before and after handling food ingredients. The cruciality of maintaining the hygiene by handwashing is a crucial standard to maintain in your business. This also affects all employees, not only the cooking staff. Handwashing is mainly required by those staff who would be handling money. Generally, handwashing is a normal hygiene practice for everyone. If you have kept this practice before now, it will be way easier for you to maintain this in your business.

- Properly store food in refrigerators: food is expected to be stored at a frequency of 40F or any lower frequency. This frequency rate helps to reduce the growth of bacteria in the food or vegetables. A refrigerator with poor frequency will encourage bacterial growth and cause your food to get stale early. Also, note that there is some type of food that you cannot keep in the refrigerator for long before it starts to lose its nutrient and get stale. Hence, endeavor to pay attention to the expiry date of canned or packaged products before refrigerating them.

- Sanitization of preparation equipment and work surfaces: contamination could also occur through dirty work surfaces and utensils. Take proper time to clean all your utensils, cutting boards, kettles, pots, pans, and everything that gets to have contact with the food.

- Get familiar with local health codes in your district: when you understand the trivialities of your district health codes, it helps you devise an effective strategy to help you align with the requirements in the code. Take proper note of all indicated regulations and do everything in your might to abide by them to keep your business running effectively.

- Use a reliable thermometer: poor temperature could affect the productivity of your staff and lead to the spread of bacteria-like microorganisms. Temperature control could be challenging. Hence, ensure to secure an effective thermometer.

- Wash! wash!! Wash!: don't ever leave your produce for a night without washing it. You are sure to have bacteria outbreaks which are near siblings to food poisoning outbreaks. One downside is that these bacteria cannot be seen by just observing the produce. Hence, make it a habit of washing every washable ingredient you will use in preparing your menu.

Finally, you can never care too much. Devise a workable storage strategy that will eliminate the spread of illness-causing bacteria, rodents' invasion, and other pests. Keep to the health regulations and ensure your employees do so also.

Chapter 9

Assemble and Manage Your Team

As a small business, a food truck is a really good way to train your hands-on business skills and test run your ability to manage people and situations. In the food truck business, it is expected that you hire staff a month or three weeks before launching your business. Also, you have to be keen on hiring staff that would be willing to stay for a time long enough before moving on to somewhere else. This is so because it takes a lot to train a staff to get familiar with the business and the nature of work that is done. You can't keep changing and staffing people every season. Foodtruck is one of those businesses that expect you to stay proactive and uptight on your management ability.

You must have all staff on deck before commencing the business and be smart enough to recruit another when a vacancy pops up.

Here is a list of hires you might need to make to have your business standing firmly;

Food Truck Manager

This is the first hire you are expected to make because it helps you coordinate other staff and contribute to the hiring decisions. The manager needs to be a smart, energized, and independent organizer of your business activities who is cool with working at speed. He/she is the beat of the business. They call the shots after you and bring decisions to reality or deliberations to business situations. They are to be really positive individuals amid business storms. These are the kind of virtues that rubs off on the mood of the workplace and the joy of the staff members. A depressed or sadist manager will turn out to be an angry person shouting back and forth, making unnecessary complaints at all times. It is a big win for you if you can get someone to beat that.

As a food truck manager, your staff is expected to be able to carry out the following tasks;

- Day to day operations
- Training of recruited staff
- Ensuring staff members are hygiene and sanitation conscious
- Adhere to outlined health regulations

- Financial management
- Truck driving service.

However, it is important that you pass a driver record check before hiring to be certain that your manager has the required license and clean record to drive your truck.

Determine The Number of Staff You Need

The window of staff that can work in a food truck at a time is within 2-6 people, depending on the truck's size. Here are some roles they could fill in;

- Chef
- Kitchen assistant
- Cooks
- Service window attendants

You can hire staffs who are willing to multi-task and are relatively good at it. Their roles could be tagged general food truck crew.

List Their Job Description

Your job description is aimed at informing your staff of their expected responsibility and the terms of employment. Also, it helps to illustrate and exposit what the nature of work is.

- Mobility of the food truck (is staff willing to travel to a different location for a few days)
- Weight lifting
- Working in a cranked-up small space
- Turning in hours after hours of work
- Driver's license

In the job description, you are also to list out employee benefits as a motivational factor in light of the expected responsibility;

- Wages or salary (state how much)
- Training
- Free working days
- Free food
- Free healthcare services

Advertise Your Job Openings

This is the hook in fishing for great staff members. You can drop a flyer or sticker on public notice boards to attract the attention of job seekers. It is much easier if you had a fixed location, so you would just place the employment vacancy on your business window.

You can put your phone number in the flyer, the vacant position, and the requirements for employment.

You could also take advantage of the online space to push for employees to fill in vacant offices. Some cities have job boards and communities online for job seekers; you can take advantage of that and post your advert there. If it is a periodic offer, you can consider hiring students.

Using online applications like an applicant tracking system makes it easy for you to sort through applications faster.

Set Up Interviews

Since you don't have a physical office location aside from the truck, which is not really a conducive place to hold an interview, you would have to hire a spot at a local business office. You could strike a bargain with them over that. Better still, you could save money, stress, and time by using an online video website for the interview.

You could do it the fun way if you have some extra bucks and host a hiring party. You could give free snacks to all applicants at this party and interview them right in front of the truck. This is also a very nice way of marketing your business.

Remember to assess the applicant's ability to work in a team and multi-task in an environment that is fast-paced.

Begin Onboarding

Take your time through the interview process, because as we said, you cannot afford to keep hiring new staff every once in a while, except you are working in seasons. Hence, you need to be relaxed and unpressured to look out for only the best. Ensure that they are familiar with the required terms of service and the regulations guiding the business. Also, look out for their willingness to take up the challenge and manage tough scenarios. At the end of the day, you must have identified a few persons that you would be recruiting.

A hygiene test could be conducted to review their thoughts on the practice of good hygiene.

After the selection process, you can begin to get them through the paperwork of filing in their biodata, alongside the required licenses and permits, like work permits. Then your training should start afterward.

Don't take too much time between advertising, interviewing, and hiring. The time frame should be closed up, and if possible, assembling your team should be done within three weeks or one month.

Chapter 10

Marketing Your Food Truck Business

The food truck business requires serious marketing to bring in profit. When you add a good marketing strategy to your food truck business plan, it makes you outstanding and helps you to attract customers. A tough marketing strategy is the key to drawing your audience to your service counter. Here is a little expo on what a well-cooked marketing strategy does for you.; it helps people identify and retain your customers. It can also give you a place above your competitors.

Below are 9 solid marketing strategies you can use;

Branding

The food industry is growing wild in a very good way; you would have to be a little wild if you will own a spot. Branding is a strategy that makes you distinguishable from other businesses. The elements listed below make up strong food truck branding strategies.

- Logo: choose a logo that depicts what menu your business sells.

- Font: creativity has its way of spicing up things. A creative font will arouse the interest of your audience. It is catchy, fun inditing and simply inviting.
- Graphics: you could create a beautiful design concept with a graphics designs tool and put it on your vehicle. This is sensational in its way and inviting. If you don't have good design skills, you can learn or hire someone to do it for you for a certain affordable fee.
- Copies: copies are to words, what advertisement is to speech. You can hire a copywriter to write you periodic copies to be uploaded on your social media. Learning the skill for yourself could save you a lot of fortune.

Website Development

A website is like an online home for your business. Although it could cost a lot of money, some cities allow for free site hosting for a while before selling it at their usual amount. Nonetheless, this shouldn't really be an alternative; you should most certainly host your website online before someone else does that with your business name. Here are things you can do to increase your responsiveness to your customers online;

- You can share your location schedule on the website so customers can know where you will be selling at over a period of time and come around there if they wish.
- Menu: upload your menu content online; you don't know whose interest it could spark. Information is like baits; it keeps calling until there is a response.
- Typical work hours: this is a strategy to announce your availability at certain locations at different times. If you'll be in the street in Los Angeles, just post day and time. Also, indicate your opening and closing work time.
- Mission statement: one of the strong reasons people consider opening a food truck is to make consumption easier and provide people with what they want as quickly as they can get it. You can write this on your page to inform people of your motives behind the business; it is a motivational factor also.

- Your food images: pictures are forever trusted shreds of evidence except in a time like ours where pictures can be easily photoshopped with no trace whatsoever. Taking and posting pictures of a satisfied consumer collecting her food, your diligent staff working, the food preparation procedures and the food in itself are some of the images you can incorporate as part of your food images.

Social Media Marketing

Social media is a gift to food truck vendors if you know how to use it. Here are some strategies you can use under social media marketing:

1. Reviews: this involves managing the comments, or reviews customer drops for you online. You can encourage your customers to drop their reviews about your menu online.
2. Two-way communications: you could build a real relationship with your customers online by posing questions to them. Questions that can you in taking decisions in your business. Common questions to ask are on locations to visit, specials

for the day, and others. It has a way of announcing your business and modifying it.
3. Photos: you can post pictures on your social media platform with enticing captions to trap people on your serving list.
4. Giveaways: this is a strategy you could use to pull the interest of people of different statuses in making decisions. You can share these giveaways on the business' webpage or your social media. You can make it a little bit exciting by making it a competition. Then the winner gains the giveaway token.
5. Let consumers mobilize people for you: you can request your customers to post a picture of their orders when they receive them. You can motivate them to post it on their social media handles and ask them to tag you to the post.

Top Social Media Platforms

Yelp: this is a social media platform where people upload their businesses and get reviews. You don't necessarily need to set up an account, all you need to do is upload details about your business, pictures inclusive, and you will find people dropping reviews for you. This site was intentionally created to help people market their business for free. Here are ways to take advantage of this platform;

1. Encourage reviews from your customers; you can place a "find us on Yelp" sticker on your truck and talk with your customers about going there to drop their reviews.
2. Include your own photos: the images on the app are usually blurry and very poor. You can upload your own food images with a very bright camera.
3. Price range: people expect food truck meals to be affordable than the usual brick and mortar. Hence endeavor to upload your prices with this consideration in mind.

Facebook: this platform is popular for its wide coverage and the number of people who use it. You can upload information on your business model, encourage people to come and patronize you, and build a sustainable relationship with your customers. You can maximize Facebook using the strategy below;

- Create events: Facebook has this create events icon that you can use to announce your location,

especially on a day you are offering discounts and specials.
- Answer all posed questions: when you create a Facebook page for your business, the structure of the page gives the audience or other users the chance to ask you questions. When you see these questions, your ability to respond quickly helps in growing your business presence online.

Twitter: the power of Twitter to boost business was formally underestimated until a very successful food truck business, Kogi, hit a breakthrough with Twitter. You can establish your business brand and a solid relationship with customers. Below are structured ways to use Twitter to your benefit;

- Make updated posts: always post information regarding your business on the site. You can give them hints on your location schedule and your available supplies.
- Share your brand: Twitter is one of the best places for you to implore originality and creativity. Hence, also ensure to express your brand language and identity.

Instagram: this is where you can upload a limitless number of your food images and shine. It is a photo app that allows you to share your special pictures with the world. Here is an in-depth leverage to use in benefiting your business through Instagram;

- Insta stories: which means Instagram stories. Asides from posting pictures, you can use it to raise a discussion as regards your business. You can throw up a question and attach a giveaway with it. You could teach on the benefit of certain meals that are on your menu.
- Post and repost images: you can encourage customers to post pictures of the food; when they repost images, ensure to repost.
- Influencer marketing: there are people on Instagram with a very high number of followers. You can chat up such people and ask them to help you market your business on your level. You should prepare an expected expenses budget incase the person asks to be paid.
- Create reels: reels are brief interesting videos of different pictures with music in the background. It is very creative and really inviting. It helps increase your business visibility.

Tiktok: this is another video-based website or app. This is another place where you can drop your reels if you made Instagram reels. Open an account and start searching for successful food truck owners in your environment and follow them. Also, use hashtags that are related to your business when you want to post. You can improve your videography skills by watching other related videos. Here are ideas you can use in making your business Tiktok videos.

- Take videos of the food preparation process.
- Video your staff preparing the recipes for a food on your menu
- When you go to cater, make videos of you working at the event
- After selling up for the day, video the surrounding where you sold at or the location you'll be selling at.

Food Presentation

Implore your creativity and craft nice appealing meals that you have made at certain times. Snap and collate these images. People are ready to pay for a very beautiful and smart-looking meal. Even when you want to do food promotion, you need to take an aesthetic photo of your meal. Creating a remarkable food presentation is awesome; you can follow the guide below;

1. Photo-friendly dishware: this works like magic. Select bright-colored dishes with beautiful patterns before setting your camera. Place this plate with the food in a bright place and take your shot. White dishes give the best concept.

2. Clever containers: you can use a unique container or dishware. The latter sight will amaze you.

3. Unique garnishes: you can think of really creative garnishes that can be used, ranging from flowers to spice blends and herbs.

Food Truck App

Today there are over 25,000 food truck applications. It is majorly for the marketing of your menu items and helps you to connect to potential customers with ease. Many people use these apps to search for a food truck business nearest to them; they could be searching for you. So, browse and download a unique food truck app. Some of these apps are;

- Roaming hunger; this app is available around /Europe, China, and America. If you stay within any of these cities, create an account. It is also referred to as a food truck finder because it helps customers get information about the available food trucks and menus. It could also open you to food catering and event management opportunities.
- WTF (Where's The Foodtruck): this is also a search app for American food truckers. Once you register with your business details, this app shares these details on its Newsfeed, showing your location and encourage customers to patronize you. It also advertises your social handles and web address.
- Find your Local food truck app: most cities in developed states have their search apps that can help you find trucks that are nearest to where you stay. You can browse out these apps and sell your business on them.

Location Strategy

It is no exaggeration to say location is everything to the food truck market. Your location determines how well your business will do and how much you will be able to sell in a day. Identify the geographical location you'll love to base in and stimulate people within there with your juicy menu. You could connect local agents to find out the latest entertainment show that would be happening to beat your competitors to booking a spot on the site early.

At this point, you should realize that you can't just park your truck anywhere; you need to be legally approved and permitted to park your truck in a certain location before you do so. Although some cities can be really strict with their parking regulations, you can be sure there is still an allowance somewhere for food truckers. However, endeavor to follow these guides and regulations; it is very important for your business credit.

Food truck location ideas

It is a smart marketing strategy to take your truck around different peculiar areas in the city. This will help you ensure that many people get to know about your business and get interested in what you sell. This is also an experiment for you to identify where you are best welcomed and patronized; you can then begin to pay a frequent visit to that location. Here are a few location ideas;

1. Commercial areas with a low number of food choices
2. Popular parks
3. Farmer's markets
4. Food truck park
5. Near a campus
6. At a local event

Catering

This is a spice to food truck marketing you wouldn't want to miss. Most food truck owners don't know that they can open themselves up to a catering contract and use their truck to prepare the meal. This is a sure way to increase your clientele. Food truck catering services are patronized by most people who want to give people a different experience in their occasion.

Food truck catering clientele

The decision to partake in food truck catering is a very bold step to pushing out your brand without extra stress. You are making more money and marketing for your business at the same time. People who see you at the event will definitely want to patronize you again when they see you somewhere else.

You can cater for the following occasions;

1. Weddings
2. Official events
3. Retiree parties
4. School graduation parties
5. Conferences
6. Academic events

Partnerships

As a food truck owner, you should be open to partnerships with local organizations. While facing competition in the mobile market, partnerships would make your services unique. Organizations like schools can hire you to cater for their everyday lunch meals, and even corporate bodies can offer to partner with you to provide meals for them on an occasional basis. On very rare occasions, you could partner with other food truckers to reach a larger audience. It is a mutually beneficial relationship you can take advantage of.

Below are some partnership ideas you could apply for;

1. Food truck rallies
2. Book shops
3. Museums
4. Movie theaters
5. Sweet Food truck Team up

Merchandising

You could use your logo to run a merchandise, especially if you are certain of your fan base. When choosing to run a merchandise, ensure that your choice relates to your business closely. These are inexpensive ways to push out your brand and get customers committed to your business.

Here are a couple of ideas you can try for merchandise.

1. T-shirts
2. Lanyards
3. Stickers
4. Keychains
5. Mugs and others.

The end… almost!

Hey! We've made it to the final chapter of this book, and I hope you've enjoyed it so far.

If you have not done so yet, I would be incredibly thankful if you could take just a minute to leave a quick review on Amazon

Reviews are not easy to come by, and as an independent author with a little marketing budget, I rely on you, my readers, to leave a short review on Amazon.

Even if it is just a sentence or two!

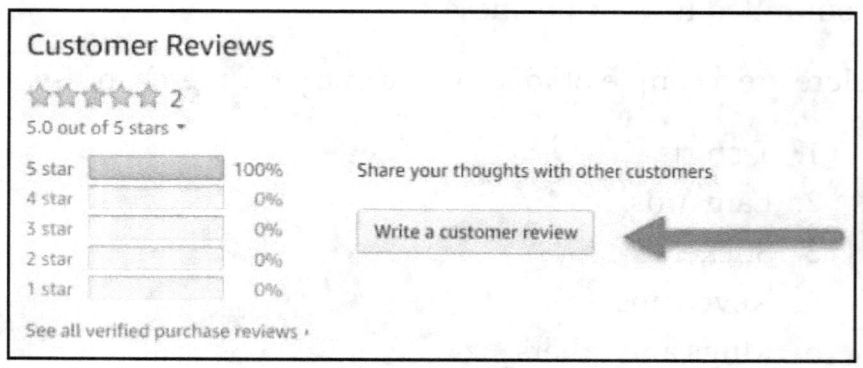

So if you really enjoyed this book, please...

\>\> Click here to leave a brief review on Amazon.

I truly appreciate your effort to leave your review, as it truly makes a huge difference

Chapter 11

Common Food Truck Mistakes To Avoid

So far, we have addressed how to make your food truck business worth the while and bring in lots of bucks as you expect it should. However, there are still a few roadblocks to achieving this feat. You'll need to avoid making the following mistakes if your business will end up a success.

- Picking the wrong truck size: the size of your truck definitely affects the daily running of your business. If you pick the wrong truck size, it is most likely that you picked a smaller truck. This can affect the running of your business. You would struggle with space to keep your equipment and work effectively. The disadvantage is inexhaustible. On the other side, you could spend a lot of money on buying a really big truck that your business model doesn't need. This is why you need to prepare a real detailed business plan that will define the space limit and size for your truck.

- Poor location graphing: you must plan your location with your customers in view. This will help you take your business to the location where your customers can easily access you and where they need it. If you build a good marketing plan, it will help you determine how to position your business to get the right quality and quantity of customers that will give you profit. You need to draft an organized plan to achieve this, so you can get a parking permit early and get people to know about your location for that period.

- Poor staff management: if you decide to work with a group of individuals as your staff, you need to create a list of requirements for staffing, so you don't get to just employ anybody. Your staffing criteria will help you structure your interview questions. Figure out how many staff members you need to function effectively, how they will fit into the schedule, and the required skills they need to have. However, you also need to have good leadership skills to motivate your employees to always be on their toes and deliver the best.

- Using a part-time approach: what this can do to your business is that it brings in a spirit of laxity and relaxation. You feel you can work only when you feel like and for the number of hours you decide to without necessarily taking into account other key considerations. This is not good at all for a food truck business. You need to be motivated to work hard. Take your business like an office job where you have to report to the office every day. Take time to make necessary preparations, go shopping, marketing, and perform all imperative paperwork. If you would have a successful food truck business, you need to be committed to taking the grind, not just cooking and serving; there is much more than that that needs to be done. If you have this amount of drive and commitment, you will not struggle to motivate your staff members to work.

- Sidelining some business activities: as mentioned in the introduction, the ability to manage a food truck business successfully is a sign that you can manage any other business if you set your mind to it. Therefore, you have to lo0k beyond standing at the front end of the business to being everywhere because every part of your business is important. If you can't monitor all of the activities, pay someone to do so. You should have a staff handling the phone calls, applying for permits for new locations, signing up for issuance of licenses, managing the business social media accounts. No stone must be left unturned. No side of the business is less important so take your time to make each of them count.

- Poor customer appreciation: one mark of good customer service is customer appreciation because the customer is king and should be treated as a king. Appreciate their patronage and see them come back a second time. If there is any problem complained about, look into it until it is settled and ensure they are satisfied; failure to do so could lead to the failure of your business.

- Dirty and disorganized workplace: cleanliness is a great trademark of the food truck business; failure to keep it is a sign of trouble. You could end up in trouble with the health officers who come for periodic inspection or lose your customer's faith in you, as they would find it difficult to entrust their safety in your meal. Also, if you are not organized with other duties like social media, online marketing, and payment of bills, it could complicate things for the business and put you at a bad risk.

- Trying to satisfy everyone: before creating your menu, it is advised that you seek the opinion of friends and family. However, if you end up receiving 20 different opinions, it is left for you to decide with your discretion which of the opinions would fit into your menu. You can't cater to everyone; you can't satisfy everyone by trying to dish all types of meal. You'll end up frustrating yourself. Choose a niche, and create your menu around it.

- A poorly designed business plan: when structuring your business plan, have the goals you intend to achieve at the corner of your mind. Your business plan should be structured around measurable goals. These goals help to keep you in check and see to it that you are on track. Be realistic about your challenges and limitations, also be keen on finding solutions to solve them through. If you find it difficult structuring your business plan, you can implore the services of a content creator. Just a side benefit you need to know, a good business plan will secure your permits early.

- Underestimating your start-up cost: this still falls back to your business plan. You ought to inquire about the cost of equipment, food truck, food ingredients, staff hire and other things before fixing your total capital. Running estimates without making inquiries is like shooting yourself in the leg because if you turn out to be wrong, you'll have a hard time making it right. A poor estimate can cripple your business and render you bankrupt at an early stage. Hence, be careful enough to make inquiries before arriving at your required startup cost.

- Making obscure expectations: one of the most obscure expectations people tend to make is expecting the business to pour out money in bucks after investing a lot. It is not bad to have high expectations. However, stay realistic. The time it will take for your business to achieve high profits is dependent on several factors. Don't start a business with all of your money and expect that it will give you all your returns in the short run. It might take a while for you to have that return. Hold a substantial amount at hand to sustain yourself and meet unforeseen expenses even after establishing the business. The profit might not come that speedily.

- Purchasing cheap equipment: high-quality equipment could be really costly; however, it is the best option you could opt for. Choosing low-quality equipment that is much more affordable could cause you to spend more money in the long run. It might seem like nothing until you sum it up. You'll find yourself spending money on repairs, consistent maintenance, and changing equipment parts. You could save yourself the extra money and stress by buying quality equipment that you are certain you can rely on.

- Not having formal recipes: when you fail to prepare your recipes for every meal and document it, you could end up producing meals with different flavors and spices every time. Consistency in taste, texture, and design requires consistent recipes. No customer will be delighted to get a different taste of the same meal at different times. Create your recipe and store it up somewhere so that when you employ a cooking staff, they can use it to continue maintaining the taste you created.

Conclusion

The challenge of managing an establishment could be way reduced if you set it up the right way. This is what this book has taken you through; how to set up a food truck business amidst unfavorable situations and still maintain top-notch creativity and service delivery. The knowledge encapsulated in this book is a top-level insight many failed food truck businesses missed that resulted in their failure. You have to be diligent and disciplined enough to hold your foot down on the ground for long. However, one bad thing you'd be doing to yourself is taking this business as a project to achieve. It is not supposed to be. Allow yourself to enjoy the building process; you might not get the chance to build anything this fun in your entire lifetime. Establishing, owning, and managing a food truck business can be a lot of work. Still, it can also be fun and adventurous, such as the road trips you'd embark on, meeting different types of customers and personalities you will encounter, devising pricing and marketing strategy to use, finding solutions to problems, and of course, the highlight of the whole business; the culinary experience.

This is a wholesome package you shouldn't miss out on; allow yourself to enjoy the moment, the business, and the experiences, and while at it, ensure to adhere to the knowledge shared in this book for the best possible result in your food truck business.

References

Financial, F. (2018, July 2). *Pros and Cons of Opening a Food Truck Business*. Fora Financial. https://www.forafinancial.com/blog/industries-we-serve/pros-cons-opening-food-truck-business/

D, G. (2021, April 23). *How To Name Your Food Truck*. Street Food Central. http://streetfoodcentral.com/how-to-name-your-food-truck/

Guillory, S. (2020, June 25). *What You Need to Know About Food Truck Financing*. Nav. https://www.nav.com/blog/food-truck-financing-544156/

Nightingale, J. (2014, December 11). *How Successful Food Trucks Choose the Best. . .* Restaurant Engine. https://restaurantengine.com/food-trucks-choose-best-locations/

W. (2021b, July 1). *How to Write a Food Truck Business Plan.* WebstaurantStore. https://www.webstaurantstore.com/article/54/how-write-food-truck-business-plan.html

W. (2021b, June 15). *The Ultimate Guide to Food Truck Marketing.* WebstaurantStore. https://www.webstaurantstore.com/article/146/food-truck-marketing.html

S. (2021a, March 10). *7 Mistakes to Avoid When Running a Food Truck - Zac's Burgers*. Zac's Burgers. https://zacsburgers.com/mistakes-to-avoid-when-running-a-food-truck/

Cuisine, M. (2018, May 25). *7 Things To Consider When Choosing A Food Truck*. Mobile Cuisine | Food Truck, Pop Up & Street Food Coverage. https://mobile-cuisine.com/startup-basics/choosing-a-food-truck/

Say, M. (2015, July 9). *The Legal Ins And Outs Of Starting A Food Truck*. Forbes. https://www.forbes.com/sites/groupthink/2015/07

/09/the-legal-ins-and-outs-of-starting-a-food-truck/?sh=239700ff23b2